Veil and Lipstick

Three Modern Arab Women Writers

Wijdan Alsayegh & Thomas Zimmerman

Near Eastern Studies Department
University of Michigan

English Department
Washtenaw Community College

1

CONTENTS

ACKNOWLEDGMENTS

Portions of this book were first published, in slightly different form, on the blog of the online journal *Asymptote* on 15 June 2017, 10 July 2017, and 25 October 2017.

INTRODUCTION

Why *Veil and Lipstick?*

The title reflects the nature of the world of women in Arab society, noting that both the veil, or *burqa* (usually black), and lipstick (usually red) are specific details in the lives of women in general and Arab women in particular. Lipstick suggests the artificial beauty that conceals the natural beauty and features of the face, and the burqa hides a large area of the face. Both veil and lipstick highlight the surface aspects of a woman and not the spiritual side. The more profound meanings here are lipstick as a symbol of patriarchal society's idea of a sexually alluring woman and as this society's habit of beautifying ugly truths. The veil, or burqa, operates as a symbol of the society's desire to cover a woman's sinful body and, by covering it, to own it as property. The veil also symbolizes the society's need to hide the reality of women's lives behind traditional patriarchy.

At first glance, the relationship between lipstick and veil appears paradoxical. The society desires women as sexual objects yet hides this sexuality from society at large by covering the objectified female body and face, reserving it for whomever might own it. Thus, lipstick and veil reveal the connection between women and patriarchal society--that is, lipstick as seductive body and veil as objectified and owned female body that is a follower but not followed, that is a body and not a brain. This is true of the nature of social issues and the Arab culture's treatment of them as they are either decorated or artificially beautified and far from reality, or covered and hidden behind the burqa of the justifications and outdated customs that allow them. These are the issues discussed in this book

Have Arab female writers succeeded in liberating themselves from the culture of lipstick and burqa to bravely reflect the details of their society without makeup and without hiding? It is a complex endeavor, but the Arab women's movement has succeeded in trying to solve this dilemma by putting readers face to face with taboo social issues that plague Arab society and still need to be amended and corrected. Arab male writers have hesitated to discuss these issues under a barrage of taboos and sociopolitical pressures. The corrections sought by Arab female writers are to the patriarchal mindset, by exposing the essence of Arab cultural reality.

This book is part critical study and part introduction to three important female Arab fiction writers who are not well known to American audiences: Zainab Hefny, Huda Al-Attas, and Buthaina Khudr Makki. These brave writers shed light on dark aspects of their cultures that have not been addressed in detail before. You will not find these writers' works on any library shelves in America because these shelves are crowded by specific Arab writers whose works are translated for commercial or specifically Arab political reasons. The three women who are the subject of this book are skilled Arab activists and writers who are leading a creative movement in Arab countries that have different cultures. Though the settings of these writers' works are vivid and specific, the theme of the struggle against the "triple taboo" of sex, religion, and politics is universal because it is a struggle for human rights and human dignity.

Our focus in this book is less on the literary technique than on the content of these writers' works. We will discuss important and controversial aspects of religion, politics, gender, and sexuality in Arab society. Religious studies, political studies, sociological studies, racial studies, gender studies, women's studies, and Middle Eastern studies are some of the categories that this book might fall into. These themes are intertwined in Arab culture, and these three writers depict this complexity in their work. For example, Saudi writer Zainab Hefny presents, in her novel *A Pillow for Your Love*, the most hidden, controversial issue in Arab countries, specifically in Saudi Arabia: the Sunni-Shiite conflict, which, as Hefny makes clear, is not only religious but only also political, social, and racial. The same complex dynamic appears in Black Arab Buthaina Khudr Makki's novel *Ankle Bracelet of Thorns*, which discusses the discrimination against Black Arabs in Arab countries, particularly Saudi Arabia. Similarly, Yemeni writer Huda al-Attas, in her collected stories, *Three Steps*, sheds light on patriarchal oppression of women and matches form with content by presenting an innovative female-voiced genre of writing that is as freeing artistically as it is thematically.

This book is the first in a projected series of books that will reveal the underrepresented voices of highly skilled creative Arab writers outside the accepted political agenda who are bravely challenging injustice in their cultures. It is our hope that reading this book will open readers' minds and hearts.

CHAPTER 1

ARAB WOMEN'S WRITING AND RELIGIOUS TABOOS: ZAINAB HEFNY

(1)

Women Writers in Saudi Society

Despite the dominant conservative society of Saudi Arabia, the Saudi creative scene is considered the most daring in the Arab region. Indeed, many Saudi writers are courageous enough to confront the power of a patriarchal, religious culture; however, some have paid the price for their opinions, bold visions, and enlightened thoughts. For instance, liberal journalist and novelist Dr. Turki Al Hamad was known for his hard line against the Wahhabi order of the Minister of the Interior following a complaint filed by religious authorities in December 2012 because of his tweets that were considered offensive to the divine, to Islam, and to the Prophet Muhammad. One such tweet states, "A new Nazi view of the world the Arab world calls Islamism. But this time of Nazism is over, and the sun will shine again" (1). Even more recently, the Saudi writer Raif Badawi was sentenced to ten years' imprisonment and floggings as punishment for using writing to express and expose the need for societal change (2).

This atmosphere applies as well to the women's creative scene in Saudi Arabia. In the recent wave of female writers such as Raja Al Sanea, Raja Alem, Samar Al Mogren, and Badria Al-Bishr daring to discuss the social taboos and the patriarchal rule of their society with courage to reveal the hidden details, we find Zainab Hefny, novelist (3) and short story (4) writer, speaking clearly. Hefny draws the reader's attention with her daring writing that attacks the conservative and patriarchal Saudi society. Indeed, her texts reveal the factual details of the underground workings of this society. She mentioned in one of her TV interviews that "if you want to know exactly what is going on in my society, just read my novels" (5). Furthermore, she has indicated that "Saudi women writers' texts are revolutionary because Saudi women writers had no choice but the pen to disclose their suffering due to the enormity of the social pressures" (6). Hefny has refused to wear Islamic dress, including the hijab and burqa [scarf and veil], during media interviews and press appearances in newspapers and journals. She says about the hijab and burqa, "I realized that a lot of social heritage is not based in *sharia* [Islamic law], but the link between the two has become taken for granted with the succession of time. Now, it is difficult for any individual in our society that comes out of the shell of the cultural norms to escape extreme actions such as reprimands in the form of the ugliest charges or even being stoned (7).

Within the Arab world, Hefny is identified with two Arab icons, Egyptian feminists Hoda Shaarawi (1879-1947) and Dr. Nawal El Saadawi (1930-). Shaarawi was an earlier feminist who took a similar unpopular position on the burqa, and Saadawi is known for her strong support of women's issues against a patriarchal society. Hefny has said, "I am proud of my new nicknames, the Saudi Shaarawi and the Saudi Nawal Saadawi, because these women courageously stood for women's issues, and I am proud today to stand in my writings against the perception of the inferiority of women as evil objects who must be domesticated so as not to sabotage the community" (8).

Hefny's writing journey began at the age of twelve, when she had her first work published. She remembered her father's reaction when she told him about her first publication: "I was running happily to show him my published text. When he looked at my name published in the journal, his eyes filled with tears of joy" (9). In contrast, there was a more strained relationship with her mother, which Hefny describes in one of her autobiographical texts: "When I arrived at the point of womanhood and the world of femininity rushed at me, I hurried excitedly to tell my mother that my period had come. I chattered on that I am like her now. My mother pulled me to her, hugging and kissing me. I passed that night dreaming about entering this new world where I am able to wear makeup and high heels. The next day, I was surprised when my mother brought me an abaya [black cloak] to put on any time I left the house. I asked her, 'Why?! What is the reason?!' She said, 'You've become a bride.' I replied, asking her, 'Where is the groom, my mother?!' My mom smiled and said, 'He will definitely come one day.' I took the cloak and stuffed it into the closet. Suddenly, I was overcome by a crazy idea to go out and leave the cloak behind. I tried to do that immediately. I found my mother rushing toward me, glaring at me, and threatening to tell my father that I had committed this crime. She told me angrily, "Do you want wagging tongues to ruin our reputation?" (10).

Hefny's marriage did not last long. The death of her husband left her alone to deal with raising their children and all the other family responsibilities in a society that oppresses women and believes in masculine tutelage. In 2004, she wrote, "Our society insists on the treatment of women as unqualified creatures who need masculine tutelage to be imposed upon them. Women are forbidden to travel outside the country without a male guardian, and their educational path from the school to the university is also subject to the approval of a male guardian. Women have no right to even get an ID card or passport without a formal letter from a male guardian. There are a lot of jobs that are still limited to men and are unavailable to women, under the pretext of fear that this kind of intellectual tolerance will lead to social disintegration! Next, women are deprived of the right of driving a car but are allowed to ride alone with a male driver, even one who is a stranger. All of the disparate media channels are managed by men. If we look at the written press, we will find that the Saudi female journalists are far away from decision-making, and none of them, regardless of journalistic success abroad, occupy the position of editor-in-chief, even in local newspapers. If women have the somewhat lower position of managing editor, they still lack the authority to change even the location of an advertisement in their newspaper! Moving on to the audio-visual media, we find that female announcers shackled to certain programs are contracted with them for low wages, and are not on the career path as men are, thus ensuring a purely masculine Saudi society. These facts lead to a restriction of women's upward mobility, forcing women to stand at the ends of lines until a man feels generous enough to clear the closed path in front of them. A woman's good or bad luck is determined by the cruel mercy of men, who have all the power. Because of this, the palace of women's dreams is destroyed by men who take advantage of their authority and pretend that they are protective guardians staying alert to offer comfort and safety. This leads women to raise the flag of surrender and to obey completely" (11).

Hefny has described her contradictory life existing under this masculine culture: "I suffered from emotional deprivation after my husband's death, but God compensated me with the gift of writing. On paper, I fell in love with whom I wanted. On paper, I chose the man I married. On paper, I divorced whom I didn't want" (12). Due to her bold writing about sensitive topics in her society, Hefny's books have been banned from participation in book fairs that are held in Saudi Arabia (13). Moreover, her books have not been published, and she has been excluded from any public literary events in Saudi Arabia. For example, in one of her television interviews, she described how "my literature has been ignored in Saudi Arabia, where I have not been called to any conference about the novel in my homeland. I want to share a funny story: I got an official invitation to present my creative testimony about my writing at a conference on the novel in my city, Jeddah. Then three days later, I received a formal apology indicating that I had been invited by mistake and I would no longer be included. That hurt me a lot, and I contacted the Minister at that time, but his answer was polite while he still did not give me the real reason" (14).

Because of her collection of short stories, *Women at the Equator* (1996), which discussed and highlighted social themes in Saudi society, including women's political rights and lesbian relationships, Hefny was prevented from writing and traveling abroad. She has said in this regard, "It is usual for the State to react violently because I publicly announced the scandals of the community, but I personally find that this collection of short stories was ahead of its time because the stories discussed the freedoms of Saudi people, including their right to representation by a Parliament as well as the right of women to drive a car" (15). She added, "I know that the real writer is a writer who writes for a change in society and any change in a society is born of violent reactions and will be in the face of clashes, and I am used to paying the price." She asserted further, "The good writer is not a writer who highlights the positives in the community and writes to please everyone. Instead, a good writer writes for us to know our mistakes and face them. Our real problem lies in Arab habits that prefer to cover up social problems without facing them" (16).

Over the course of her career, Hefny has faced a barrage of charges. First, that a man, not she, is the original author of her writing, to which she replied, "I used to hear this charge a lot, especially since the prevailing view of women writers was that their pens were too weak to write about rugged topics and they were not entitled to write boldly" (17). She added, "I wrote boldly while discussing political and social issues, which usually men write about" (18). Another accusation leveled at her is that her fiction contains autobiographical material and that her heroines are but different faces of the writer herself. In fact, the well-known television broadcaster Turki al-Dakhil, host of the program *Adaat* [*Lightings*], criticized her judgmentally for this, to which she replied, "The heroines of my novels are not Zainab Hefney." (19) She explained, "Creative writing occupies an insane realm in which I enter a prohibited area with my fictional characters and leave them to follow their own nature" (20). Yet another accusation is that she has used sex to sell her books, a common marketing strategy. She replied to this by saying, "I have used sex in my writing for noble goals and to discuss realistic social situations" (21). She added, "Sex is an important part of our lives, but sexual taboos were not present in our ancient history. In the past, we had an intellectual civilization because the writer was free. Now, we have actually regressed religiously and socially. For example, today there is cultural and religious apostasy because Andalusian books, such as *Ṭawq al-Ḥamāmah* [*The Ring of the Dove*] (22), would not be published today, and if a contemporary female poet were to recite, for example, these lines from Andalusian poet Wallada bint al-Mustakfi (1093 AC) (23), 'I allow my lover to touch my cheek / And offer my kiss to whomever craves it,' she would be stoned" (24).

Hefny has responded to the idea that real literature is literature that respects the nature of the conservative society and its sense of morality by saying, "We cannot apply this criterion to literature because the writing itself is not moral when it dives deeply into prohibited areas to reveal the nakedness of an immoral society." She added, "We use the term 'conservative society' to cover our double standard" (25). She added further, "Our society prohibits women from having even the most basic rights" (26). She mentioned, "Women live in violation, and there are no institutions to protect them" (27). She added, "Our society is a macho society that has distorted history in men's favor and handcuffed the progress of society" (28). She said about the situation of women in Saudi Arabia, "Unfortunately, the religious culture of Wahhabism has contributed to blocking of the progress of women, and the growing demand for the necessity of gender segregation after the Grand Mosque seizure in 1979 led to mounting religious extremism and the dominance of hardline religious discourse over all aspects of life in Saudi Arabia, especially women's from A to Z, relying on only the Wahhabi family interpretation of doctrine as legislation. As religious radio and television programs intensify, as do fatwas which are based on intimidation and prohibition (*haram/halal*), women have been marginalized and excluded from public life! This interpretation rejected the idea of women taking a leading position and included the promotion of a prophetic saying, 'No people shall ever prosper who appoint a woman as their ruler.' This cast doubt on women's intellectual capacity and presented the image of women as creatures that will lead to the spread of corruption in society if they are left without supervision and are not always under the tutelage of a man!" (29). She added, "Saudi feminist literature is revolutionary par excellence because women writers under such social stress have nothing but their pens to expose it." She added proudly, "I am the first of the sexual revolution on paper in Saudi Arabia" (30).

Hefny has described the duality of social taboos in real life and freedom in fictional life: "I have my mother's warnings firmly in my intellectual mind, but when I create fictional female characters in my short stories and novels, I have fun and dance with them. I stick my tongue out at my society's taboos, and I say, 'Look at me. I created my own woman characters who are able to stand before you, fight against you, and you don't have any power to judge them, or report them to the police station, or destroy their reputation, or even prevent them from living their realistic love story in broad daylight" (31).

Hefny currently writes a column in the United Arab Emirates newspaper Al Ittihad [United] and discusses freely political and social issues. She has said, "I did not participate in the press in Saudi Arabia because the ceiling for freedom is still low (32) and also because I do not like the censor's red pen" (33). However, her bold thoughts were published in a weekly column in a Saudi newspaper that was published in London during her residency there, but she said, "I was discharged from work without a clear reason" (34).

Her writing boldly discusses various taboos in Saudi Arabia, such as women's rights, male guardianship, domestic violence, homosexuality, forbidden sexual relations, and social and sectarian racism. Furthermore, her writings have been published throughout many Arab countries, such as Egypt, Lebanon, and Syria, but she has not been successful in having any book published in Saudi Arabia. She answered the interviewer who questioned her regarding this, "Give me one publisher who will accept my books" (35).

Finally, Zainab Hefny, through her creative experience which has spanned more than two decades, has not bowed in her writings and positions to the glamor of fame, money, or career advancement, but vowed the same principle of seeking to liberate the positions of Saudi women from the clutches of religious authority that is dedicated to a culture of marginalization of women. Through this, Hefny has brought us back to literature committed to human issues concerning men and women. Her calculated audacity, even though it has resulted in sanctions such as banned books, travel restrictions, and denial of participation in book exhibitions, still fuels her project to improve the human condition through a literature of commitment.

References

(1) Fakhri Saleh, "Freedom for the Thinker Novelist Turki Al-Hamad," *Addustour* [Jordanian newspaper], No. 17 257 Year 49, 1 Aug. 2015.
(2) "Saudi Blogger Receives First 50 Lashes of Sentence for 'Insulting Islam.'" *The Guardian*, 10 Jan. 2015, https://www.theguardian.com/world/2015/jan/09/saudi-blogger-first-lashes-raif-badawi
(3) Zainab Hefny, *Dance to the Tambourine* [novel] (Cairo: Arab Record Publishing House, 1998).
---, *I've No Longer Cried* [novel](London: Dar Al-Saqi, 2004).
---, *Features* [novel](London: Dar Al-Saqi, 2006).□
---, *Crooked Legs* [novel](Lebanon: Arab Institute for Studies and Publication, 2008).
---, *A Pillow for Your Love* [novel] (London: Dar Al-Saqi, 2011).□□
(4) Zainab Hefny, *Your Restriction or My Freedom* [short stories] (Lebanon: Lebanese Arab Institution, 1994).
---, *Women at the Equator* [short stories] (Cairo: Sunrise Publishing House, 1996).
---, *There Are Things That Disappear* [short stories] (Lebanon: Dar Al- Rayes, 2000).
(5) LBC, Lebanon Public TV Channel, *Ms. Program*, Assma Wahbah, 18 July 2014. https://www.youtube.com/watch?v=RRWnfSKODGg

(6) Ibid.

(7) Zainab Hefny, "My Story with the Letter," Women's Forum and Writing, Morocco, July 2004 .

(8) Al Arabiya , a Saudi TV channel, *Adaat* program by Turki Al- Dakheel, 25 Nov. 2011, https://www.youtube.com/watch?v=Ox8_SyyyJlk

(9) LBC, Lebanon Public TV Channel, *Ms. Program*, Assma Wahbah, 18 July 2014, https://www.youtube.com/watch?v=RRWnfSKODGg

(10) Zainab Hefny, "My Story with the Letter," Women's Forum and Writing, Morocco, July 2004.

(11) Ibid.

(12) LBC, Lebanon Public TV Channel, *Ms. Program*, Assma Wahbah, 18 July 2014, https://www.youtube.com/watch?v=RRWnfSKODGg

(13) Alhurra , Arab American TV Channel, *Gulf Dialogue Program*, Suleiman Al-Hattlan, 21 June 2014, https://www.youtube.com/watch?v=btWStb2lrJo

(14) Ibid.

(15) LBC, Lebanon Public TV Channel, *Ms. Program*, Assma Wahbah, 18 July 2014, https://www.youtube.com/watch?v=RRWnfSKODGg

(16) Al-Arabiya, a Saudi TV channel, *Adaat* program by Turki Al-Dakheel, 25 Nov. 2011, https://www.youtube.com/watch?v=Ox8_SyyyJlk

(17) Ibid.

(18) Ibid.

(19) Ibid.

(20) Alhurra , Arab American TV Channel, *Gulf Dialogue Program*, Suleiman Al Hattlan, 21 June 2014, https://www.youtube.com/watch?v=btWStb2lrJo

(21) Al-Arabiya, a Saudi TV channel, *Adaat* program by Turki Al-Dakheel, 25 Nov. 2011, https://www.youtube.com/watch?v=Ox8_SyyyJlk

(22) *The Ring of the Dove: A Treatise on the Art and Practice of Arab Love*, by Ibn Hazm (994AC- 1069AC) (Author), Anthony Arberry, 1 Jan. 1994, Luzac Oriental (May 1995). □□□□□

(23) *The Breeze of the Scent from an Andalusian Moistened Branch*, Ahmed bin Mohammed Mokri Tlemceni (1631AC), Beirut (Export Press), 1388 = 1968.

(24) Al-Arabiya, a Saudi TV channel, *Adaat* program by Turki Al-Dakheel, 25 Nov. 2011, https://www.youtube.com/watch?v=Ox8_SyyyJlk, and LBC, Lebanon Public TV Channel, *Ms. Program*, Assma Wahbah, 18 July 2014, https://www.youtube.com/watch?v=RRWnfSKODGg

(25) Al-Arabiya, a Saudi TV channel, *Adaat* program by Turki Al-Dakheel, 25 Nov, 2011, https://www.youtube.com/watch?v=Ox8_SyyyJlk

(26) Ibid.

(27) Ibid.

(28) Ibid.

(29) Zainab Hefny, "Hijazi Women Between Yesterday and Today," Graduates in Bahrain Club Hall, Bahrain, 2009.

(30) LBC, Lebanon Public TV Channel, *Ms. Program*, Assma Wahbah, 18 July 2014, https://www.youtube.com/watch?v=RRWnfSKODGg

(31) Zainab Hefny, "Testimony in Creative Experience," Sanaa Fourth Festival of the Story and the Novel, Ministry of Culture, Sanaa, 2008.

(32) Al-Arabiya, a Saudi TV channel, *Adaat* program by Turki Al-Dakheel, 25 Nov. 2011, https://www.youtube.com/watch?v=Ox8_SyyyJlk

(33) Alhurra, Arab American TV Channel, *Gulf Dialogue Program*, Suleiman Al Hattlan, 21 June 2014,
https://www.youtube.com/watch?v=btWStb2lrJo
(34) Al-Arabiya, a Saudi TV channel, *Adaat* program by Turki Al-Dakheel, 25 Nov. 2011, https://www.youtube.com/watch?v=Ox8_SyyyJlk
(35) Ibid.

Zainab Hefny's A Pillow for Your Love:
Confronting the Shiite-Sunni Sectarian Conflict

A dominant conflict in Arab society is that between the Shiite and Sunni sects of Islam. This conflict has led to violence against Shiites ranging from mass graves in southern Iraq and political marginalization in Bahrain and Saudi Arabia, to other jihadist militants, such as ISIS, that sanction mass bloodshed, confiscation of property, captivity of women, and the bombing of mosques. More recently, an Arab military alliance led by Saudi Arabia struck Shiite targets in Yemen, one of the poorest countries in the region, and left hundreds of dead and wounded as well as destruction and devastation. Despite these widespread phenomena, very few Arab writers have discussed boldly the daily suffering and violation of political rights due to this sectarian violence.

However, one who has stood up to condemn this racist sectarianism is the Sunni Saudi novelist and short story writer Zainab Hefny (1, 2). For more than twenty years, Hefny has led a bold women's movement and seeks through her writings the advancement of both society and women. She has played an important role as an activist writer who touches on social, sexual, and religious taboos, such as women's political rights and lesbianism. She goes beyond the dominant political ideology that assigns religious guardianship and fosters a patriarchal culture that shackles women. In her novel *A Pillow for Your Love* (2011), Hefny discusses religious taboos in the Arab community, including social and religious racism against the Shiite sect. In a bold manner, she highlights the plight of the Shiite sect in Saudi Sunni society, which is a thorny issue not only because of the Sunni perception of the social inferiority of the Shiite community but also because the Sunnis consider the Shiite religious outlook blasphemous. The novel discusses this dilemma through the narrative fabric, revealing the sufferings of the Shiite community as a result of that perception of inferiority and portraying how the conservative Sunni society deals with it, evidenced through the awareness of the protagonists of the novel, Jaafar (a Shiite) and Fatima (a Sunni).

The events of the novel flow smoothly to reach the meeting between Jaafar and Fatima outside their country, in Lebanon, and their involvement in a sexual relationship, which is a forbidden relationship religiously and socially and is a clear challenge to the religious and social taboos. The two lovers are physically and psychologically compatible, and at the end of the novel they get married, overcoming the obstacles that have hindered them. Hefny, in a television interview about the reason for ending the novel with the marriage of a Shiite man to a Sunni woman, said, "Intermarriage between communities is the beginning of reconciliation; our problem lies in our educational curricula that fuel sectarianism" (3).

A Pillow for Your Love successfully depicts the suffering of the Shiite community by highlighting the inferior perception that Sunni society has of it. For example, a tense scene between Fatima and Jaafar reflects the social structure based on religious racism that judges individuals based on the inferiority of their sect. The scene begins with Jaafar acknowledging his love for Fatima and his desire to marry her. This news brings great pleasure to Fatima, a widow who has been deprived of physical intimacy since the death of her husband. She has focused her life on her daughter, who has recently married and traveled with her husband to pursue postgraduate studies abroad. However, the mood shifts from the height of happiness to the depths of disappointment when Fatima discovers that Jaafar is Shiite. The same thing happens to Jaafar, whose feelings descend from the summit of ecstasy to the lowest humiliation. Here is the depiction their dialogue in the novel:

> She tried to gather the fragments of nerves, which had scattered before her eyes. She tried to cover her happiness, which had started to dance joyfully deep inside her. Suddenly, fear caught her by surprise. . . She asked him to talk a little bit about his family.
>
> He smiled purely, and said, "What do you want to know? From the moment that I met you, I've been keen to be an open book. I am from an Al Baqir family, Shiite Qatif families, and . . . ."
>
> She cut him off with an alarmed tone: "What? You are Shiite?! Why didn't you tell me this when we met yesterday?"
>
> He gulped at the insult. "Tell me the truth: is this matter so important to you?"
>
> "Even if it is not, do you think that my Sunni family would easily welcome the idea of my marrying a Shiite?" (4)

The narrative takes another detour to reflect the depth of the perceived inferiority of the Shiite sect by employing flashback techniques to reflect earlier suffering when Jaafar falls into what he thought was love with an educated Sunni woman. He experiences the heights of ecstasy, only to have his dream dashed by feelings of extreme humiliation and inferiority because of sectarian affiliation. In an interior monologue, Jaafar considers this:

> I was fascinated by the femininity flowing through the ropes of her voice as she talked with me over the phone. In the early days, her speech was mostly focused on America and the period of her life when she studied there and her dream of living in the bustling city of New York. Her nostalgia for the freedom that she breathed, as she walked in the New York streets, her continued disappointments since she returned to Saudi Arabia, and her inability to exercise and to work as a lawyer after her graduation from law school were clear. Her tone mixed with rebellion and anger toward her empty life. She was familiar with considerable political circumstances.
>
> I do not know how the conversation detoured to the history of the Shiites, Sunnis, and to the first Gulf War and to the involvement of Iran in Iraq's internal affairs and to Saudi Shiites. I do not know how to show the enthusiasm that I have and my sympathy for Shiites and with their right to ascend to high positions in the government, similar to the Sunnis.
>
> There was silence between us, breached by her voice, her tone tense, saying, "Your defense of Shiites is strange!"
>
> "Regardless of being my family, I'm talking here as a human being."

She was stunned by my response, and said, "--Why didn't you tell me that you are Shia?"

"Both Shiites and Sunnis bear witness that there is no god except Allah and that Muhammad is the Messenger of Allah."

"This is invalid what you claim. There are many fundamental differences between us. I cannot lie about history. Sorry. I do not want to talk with 'Rafidi'!"

She hung up the phone with this sharp tone and without saying bye.

I could not believe my ears. How can a young woman who studied abroad and has wide cultural experiences be so mentally reactionary? (5)

This scene and others in the novel lead the reader to the suffering of Jaafar as a human being who finds himself locked into his religious sect and shackled with restrictions and perceptions of inferiority and social persecution; for example, when the woman refers to him as *Rafidi*, she is using an abusive nickname that Sunnis use to insult Shiites, which refers to an event in Islamic history when a group of Muslims rejected legitimate Islamic authority and leadership.

Later, the narrative provides development of Jaafar's character through his rising religious and social consciousness while at the same time presenting another dimension of Shiite sectarian suffering. This occurs when Jaafar starts a blog under his own name in which he attempts to reconcile the conflict between the Shiite and Sunni sects. This is how Jaafar describes it:

I was in the twenty-fourth year of my life when a policeman knocked on the door of our house and told me to go with him to the police station. My father, alarmed, asked the policeman the reason for his call. The policeman answered that we would know more once got to the police station. My mother's tears and lamentations followed me to the doorstep.

The officer said, addressing my father, "Your son is accused of fomenting sectarian strife in the country through his own blog."

"This is a dangerous accusation, Officer. I beg you to release him, and let him write a letter of apology and shut down the blog forever."

"Sorry. This decision is beyond my authority. There are orders to keep him here for quite some time."

I remained in a room in the police station for two weeks. The officer questioned me several times to find out if there were foreign hands inciting me to adopt this direction. When I left the police station, I wrote an apology letter to shut down the blog. This experience strengthened me and urged me to be more aware. (6)

This scene makes clear the silencing of any Shiite attempts to alleviate the Shiite-Sunni strife while at the same time suggesting, with the mention of "foreign hands," that these attempts are traitorous.

Jaafar, in the following bitter monologue, expresses his sadness over injustice and oppression: "Many questions began to swell in the intellectual truth about what is going on around me. My sense of injustice began to worsen day by day. Marginalized citizen that I am within my homeland!" (7).

During the novel's events, the heated dialogues between Fatima and Jaafar reflect the contrast between the details of their two different religious doctrines' interpretations of the Qur'an, especially when they are talking about women's rights in the following narrative scene:

> "Well, Jaafar, I agree with your view, but doesn't your doctrine permit a pleasure marriage [*Nikah Al-mut'ah*], which is a big insult to women? Is marriage just a night or nights that evaporate and disappear?
>
> He laughed coolly, saying, "Hallelujah, O Fatima, but don't you think your Sunni doctrine insults women's rights too?! Doesn't your doctrine have a common-law marriage and *Misyaar* marriage, *Almesfar* marriage, *Friend* marriage, and *Weekend* marriage?! Every day your Imams have created new fatwas of marriage that don't exist in the original Islamic Sharia! Are not these marriages a denial of women's rights with their allowing, by disguising prostitution, the degradation of the status of women?" (8)

Necessarily this scene may reverse how Shiite sects and Sunni sects deal with women's rights and how each of them denies rights with doctrinal interpretations that work in favor of men at the expense of women. The scene also sheds light on the degrading stereotype that all Shiites are the illegitimate offspring of pleasure marriages (*Nikah Al-mut'ah*) while indicating that there are parallel models in the Sunni sect (*Misyaar, Mesfar, Friend,* and *Weekend*).

The novel is a reflection in more than one place of this social duality based on religious heritage in dealing with women's rights and especially the right to choose a husband in a patriarchal society that operates by a double standard. This is shown through Fatima's encounter with a friend who is newly married to a man younger than she:

> I met her by chance in one of my family visits. I did not recognize her. She seemed more youthful, her face brimming with freshness. She leaned toward me confidentially, saying, "Here is advice from an experienced woman: Don't pay attention to the words of the people. Form a bond with a man younger than you to regain your youth. Why is it the right of men to marry virgin women decades younger than they under the pretext that they follow the example of the prophet Muhammad and the notorious story of his marriage to Mrs. Aisha?! Why do they say sarcastically in our communities that a middle-aged woman who gets married to a younger man is trying to rejuvenate herself and desperately wants to live both in her time and his other time?! Is it not our right as women also to follow the example of Ms. Khadija [Prophet Muhammad's first wife]? Did she not marry the Prophet, who was fifteen years younger at the time? Don't say, but she is "the mother of Muslim believers"! She laughed out loud then followed with a certain wink: "At that time, his prophecy had not emerged yet. She desired him as a man. Isn't that true?!" (9)

The text boldly discusses the sexual needs of women and men together under social and religious taboos through Fatima, who is older than Jafaar, and through two female characters, Aisha and Khadija, who have holy positions in Islam due to their relationship to the Prophet. The bold discussion is punctuated by probing questions: "Is it not our right as women also to follow the example of Ms. Khadija?" and "Why is it the right of men to marry virgin women decades younger than they under the pretext that they follow the example of the Prophet Muhammad and the notorious story of his marriage to Mrs. Aisha?!"

Hefny highlights another plight of physical deprivation for Fatima, a widow and single mother who is addicted to masturbation as an alternative to the absence of an emotional and psychological partner. The following narrative scene employs a satirical event, the meeting between Fatima and her best friend, Fayiza, who brings her a personal device from France as a gift while she was traveling with her husband. Bringing it into the country put her reputation and marriage at risk:

> When Fayiza returned to Jeddah from one of her travels to France, she surprised me with a gift wrapped with brightly colored paper. She told me jokingly, "I brought you a groom." I opened the box in a hurry. Inside, there was a plastic pink rod with batteries.
>
> She did not give me an opportunity to comment. She winked, saying, "You can make your marriage contract tonight. I couldn't find any better gift for you than this one. I hid it under my shirt from the airport employee when he frisked my bag. If he had found it, it would be a huge scandal in front of my husband. I've risked my married life for you, oh, my precious Fatoom [the nickname of Fatima]."(10)

This scene's sexual frankness breaks social and religious taboos by openly discussing female sexuality. This scene is also a victory for the two women because Fayiza smuggles a symbol of this sexuality past two symbols of the traditional patriarchal society, one of them social (the husband) and the other political (the airport employee).

Hefny's novel reflects through different events the bitter irony of a religious heritage that allows the macho culture to serve the man but not the woman. For example, the following excerpt uses irony to highlight a female missionary, who reflects the depth of the problems of sex education that are faced by Saudi women due to their confusion between religion and culture. Specifically, it makes clear Fatima's confusion over the idea of masturbation as compensation for the absent partner and the fear of the fact that the practice is an unforgivable sin:

> While attending a religious lecture presented by a female missionary, I hope that I have the courage to ask her the question that haunts my intellect and thoughts. My question is about my right to masturbate. Do I have this right, or does this practice place me in the circle of the forbidden? As usual, my shame and shyness prevent me from asking.
>
> Finally, on one occasion, after a female missionary finished her presentation, which was about the sexual relationship between the husband and the wife, I gathered my strength and decided to ask her. When I tried to ask, another female voice interrupted and spoke up with her question:
>
> "Do I let my husband play with my breasts? Is it his right to suckle my nipples?"
>
> The missionary scowled and answered dryly, "God created this place for your babies and not the sexual dalliance of your man."
>
> A second woman spoke out and stated, "There is a question I feel embarrassed to ask. My husband insists on me . . .

his penis when he sleeps with me for more excitement. When I refuse, he swears he will marry another to get what he wants . . . I am confused. I do not know what to do!"

"His demand enters the circle of taboos."

"But Miss, I can't bear my husband acting on his word and marrying another woman."

"My dearest sister, suffering in your present life is much easier than the sufferings of the afterlife. Also, the Great Creator will reward you."

A third woman spoke up and asked, "I am a young divorced woman for several years, and I have not received my destined husband yet. What do I do to vent my sexual desire?"

"Seek help in fasting, praying, and continuously reading the Qur'an."

I sank deeper into my chair, my tongue was stuck to the roof of my mouth, and my question was silenced in my heart. (11)

It is clear that Hefny employs bitter comedy to expose the distance between the naive questions of the women and the doctrinal answers of the missionary, which create a vicious circle of confusion. In addition, such comedy violates religious taboos and points to the society's dire need for sex education, which Hefny has asked for in one of her television interviews (12).

In conclusion, the novel *A Pillow for Your Love* by the Saudi novelist Zainab Hefny is a qualitative addition to the canon of bold Arab writers attempting to expose the depth of the cultural, political, social, and religious crises in Arab society. These are thorny issues that few Arab writers have confronted out of fear of political and religious taboos or the inability to confront active radical readers. In addition, the novel highlights boldly the suffering of Shiites in Sunni Saudi society and goes beyond this by ending with the taboo-breaking marriage of the Shiite hero Jaafar to the Sunni heroine Fatima. Through this, Hefny has brought us back to literature committed to human issues concerning men and women. Her calculated audacity, even though it has resulted in sanctions such as banned books, travel restrictions, and denial of participation in book exhibitions, still fuels her project to improve the human condition through a literature of commitment. In the end, Hefny is like a bird that sings away from the rest of the flock, but her song will light the way for others to follow.

References

(1) Zainab Hefny, *Dance to the Tambourine* [novel](Cairo: Arabs Record Publishing House, 1998).

---, *I've No Longer Cried* [novel](London: Dar Al-Saqi, 2004).

---, *Features* [novel](London: Dar Al-Saqi, 2006). □

---, Crooked Legs [novel](Lebanon: Arab Institute for Studies and Publication, 2008).

---, *A Pillow for Your Love* [novel] (London: Dar Al-Saqi, 2011). □□

(2) Zainab Hefny, *Your Restriction or My Freedom* [short stories] (Lebanon: Lebanese Arab Institution, 1994).

---, *Women at the Equator* [short stories] (Cairo: Sunrise Publishing House, 1996).

---, *There Are Things That Disappear* [short stories] (Lebanon: Dar Al- Rayes, 2000).

Hefny's Website: http://www.zhauthor.com/html/cv.htm

(3): Alhurra, a United States-based Arabic-language satellite TV channel, *Gulf Dialogue Program*, Suleiman Al Hattlan, 21 June 2014,

https://www.youtube.com/watch?v=btWStb2lrJo

(4) Hefny, *A Pillow for Your Love*, p. 45

(5) Ibid., p. 71

(6) Ibid.

(7) Ibid., p. 72

(8) Ibid. p. 114

(9) Ibid., p. 49

(10) Ibid., p. 28

(11) Ibid., p. 32

(12) Al-Arabiya, a Saudi TV channel, *Adaat* Program, by Turki al Dakheel, published on Nov 25, 2011.

https://www.youtube.com/watch?v=Ox8_SyyyJlk

CHAPTER 2

ARAB WOMEN WRITERS AND RACISM:
BUTHAINA KHUDR MAKKI

In the Arab world, there is a long history of racism against black Arabs. For centuries, they have been denied basic human and civil rights. This social phenomenon dominates as a daily practice even today. This cultural discrimination has violated Black Arabs' dignity and humanity, rejected their social integration and ability to marry white-skinned Arabs, cast doubt on their status as real Arabs, and relegated them to the social status of slaves (Labbe, 2004; Mamouri, 2013). This daily suffering is contemporary, but its roots are deep in the Arab consciousness and appear in ancient Arabic literature such as oral biographies (Abu Zaid Al-Hilali), folk tales, and poems (Kathem, 2004). Perhaps the most famous is the suffering pre-Islamic black poet, Antarah bin Shedad. His suffering was due to his inferior status, which denied him his human rights because of his dark skin inherited from his black mother, Zebibah: "If I am a Black, my black came from the musk. There is no healing from my blackness" (Antarah, 1994). Antarah's white father, who was master of the tribe, looked at his own black son as a mere shepherd, ignoring his great physical strength and status as a hero who protected his tribe during wartime. This caused bitter feelings in Antarah. At one time, when his father asked him to protect the tribe from an attack by a powerful enemy, Antarah replied, "A slave does not excel in the hit (*kur*) and run (*fur*), but rather specializes in milking and preparing luggage" (p. 22). When his father heard this, he said, "Kur, and you are free." (Antarah, 1994). Antarah succeeded in gaining his political freedom when his father acknowledged that he was a legitimate son and knight of the tribe. However, even Antarah's strength could not withstand the strength of Arab culture, which would not allow him to marry his beloved white cousin, Ablah. Antarah composed the most beautiful poetry, including his Mualakah, about his love for her (Tabrizi, n.d.).

This culture did not change during the Islamic period. For example, the Prophet-poet Hassan bin Thabit connected the Arab nationality and mastery with white skin. He says, in one of his famous poems, "White faces are of generous descent, and the upturned nose denotes the highest quality" (Thabit, 1994, p. 222). This denigration of black people appears also in the Abassid poets, especially in the major Arab poet Al-Mutanabbi's poems that attack Abu al-Misk Kafur, the King of Egypt, the Levant, and Hejaz, who had black skin. Al-Mutanabbi cries in favor of the Arab belief that white skin is the color of Arabism and sovereignty and black skin is the color of slavery, particularly in the following poem, considered by many to be the greatest Arabic poem, which states sarcastically, "Who taught the black eunuch honor? / His white people? Or his knights' fathers?// Don't buy a slave unless you have a stick to beat him with. / The slaves are filthy and depressed. / If the macho whites are unable to do the honorable thing, / What should we expect from the blacks?" (p. 663).

If we look at modern Arabic literature, we will find rarely that white writers or even black writers discuss this phenomenon of anti-blackness. One black Arab writer who has bravely and boldly highlighted this hidden phenomenon is Buthaina Khudr Makki, born in Sudan in 1947.

Her novel *Ankle Bracelet of Thorns* (2004) represents a pioneering effort to highlight the dimensions of the anti-black phenomenon and the daily suffering of black Arabs, particularly black Sudanese, who are the majority population in Sudan. It should be mentioned that the dictionary meaning of "Sudan" is "black people." Additionally, the author of the Arab language dictionary, *Lisan al-Arab* [*Arab Tongue*] (n.d.), stated, "Sudan is the opposite of white people."

Makki's novel moves on several technical levels, attacking many social, political, and religious taboos. However, the main theme of the novel is the perception of inferiority held by black Arabs of African descent. This is done through the stories of the two Sudanese protagonists of the novel, Nasra and Mahjoob, and their journey from Sudan to Saudi Arabia to find work. These characters' boldness comes not only from the revelation of religious taboos and speech that refers to equality between blacks and whites but also from the novel's depiction of the Arab identity being an ankle bracelet of thorns (thus the title of the novel) for black Arabs. The intended audience of the novel is Arab readers. This brave novel provides Arabs with a new image of slavery—the slavery of Arab identity, "the ankle bracelet of thorns." The novelist, Makki, on the issue of the Arab identity, has said: "I do not feel that the Sudanese who remained in Sudan and did not emigrate will feel this Sudanese ordeal of leaving for work. They will return, echoing, 'I am Sudanese, and that is enough'"("Afra Abdel Rahman," 2013).

In this novel, readers are face to face with the ordeals of the two protagonists, Nasra and Mahjoub.

Nasra: Black Female Protagonist

She is a beautiful political activist educated at Khartoum University. She comes from a poor family. Her father was an alcoholic who would come home intoxicated every day and who granted his wife, Nasra's mother, no autonomy. Nasra has been heartbroken by her relationship with her former lover, the famous lawyer, Mehdi, who was killed by American forces during a journey to Baghdad at the Arab Journalists Center. Nasra was forced after that to marry her current husband, Marghini, who is an English teacher and widower who also got an opportunity to teach English in Saudi Arabia. They produced two daughters who study at public schools in Saudi Arabia and face daily insults because of their black skin. This scene is set through a flashback in the bloody consciousness of Nasra, who disgraced the religious and social taboos because she decided to drink wine to flee the pain of her bitter present life, which has relegated her to the slave-like status of a black person:

> She is not Arab. She suspects that after residence in Saudi Arabia, she remembered that day when her daughter was complaining to her that her classmates at school used the humiliating term *eabidah* [female slave] to describe her. She was stunned initially. . . . At her grandfather's home in Sudan, there is a long ancient transcript in a gilt frame that proves her Arab lineage, relating her descent from Abbassids and Quraishis. . . . She thought that her daughter is Arab, and her descent extended from El Abbass [the Prophet's uncle]. But to integrate with pure Arab communities that uncover her and take away her Arabism, although she is of Arab tongue and Arab culture. (p. 89)

Obviously, the heroine is aware of the tenuousness of her Arab connection. She essentially strips away her Arab identity: "She is not Arab." Furthermore, she realizes that her Arab lineage, embodied in the ancient manuscript, is merely ink on paper. In addition, she renounces her descent from Mohammed's uncle when she finds out this lineage is a falsehood. By doing this, she essentially renounces her religion.

Later, the narrative reaches its climax during the heroine's interior monologue that has at its axis the metaphor of the inferior Arab affiliation for blacks being an *Ankle Bracelet of Thorns*, thus presenting a new image of slavery within the Arab identity. In the following scene, Nasra is in fact intoxicated by alcohol, a breaking of Islamic taboo:

> "No matter . . . Absolutely it is not that important to me either," she said to herself angrily. She was proud of her hybrid existence as a black Arab. Why does she cling to her Arab lineage . . . and why is she so eager to possess it while at the same time stripping herself of her African roots if this lineage offers her only an ankle bracelet of thorns and constrains the purity of her personality and her maiden voyage?" (p. 89).

The bitter wonder in this monologue marks a detour in the heroine's character development. She has found out that her Arab affiliation is a mere a decoration that stings her (an ankle bracelet of thorns), and she must break this constraint that enslaves her to the Arab lineage, which has been suspect.

The psychological separation between the heroine and her Arab identity reaches its climax when the heroine finds herself gasping and chasing the mirage of Arab identity through imitating the model of traditional Arab beauty:

> She absolutely does not resemble women of the Arabian Peninsula in shape or soul . . . So why does she carry the burden of imitating Arab women, and put on her body pounds of fat and tons of golden jewelry? She walked slowly under her heavy weight [al wajaa and al wahl], and she slept until noon [nuuwm aldduhua], and she surrendered to an example of a beautiful Arab woman who tries to satisfy her husband with her body [chker and nker], as Ayesha, daughter of Talha! And Wiladah, daughter of Al-Mustakfi, wasn't an Arab Muslim, wasn't saying, "I make my lover caress my cheek. / I gave my kiss to anyone who desired it" (p. 89)

It is clear that the text does not only require the Arab beauty model (of obesity and gold jewelry) but also the vocabulary of beauty in Arabic poetic memory, such as *al wajaa* and *al wahl* [the walk of a woman with fat thighs] from one of Al-Ilaesha's verses in his long poem "Mualakah" (Tabrizi, n.d.) and *nuuwm aldduhaa* [lady who sleeps until noon because she has servants] from one of Amru Alqais's verses in his long historical poem "Mualakah." In addition, the text also alludes to a controversial Islamic female such as Ayesha, daughter of Talha, who had a seductive body and many husbands and the Andalusian poet Wiladah, daughter of Al-Mustakfi, who was known as a bold rebel against sexual taboos. The narrative presents these panoramic images to draw a caricature of the sensuality of Arab culture, which is centered on the woman's body and how this body surrenders to patriarchal culture when this body becomes seductive and adorned with golden jewelry to satisfy men's desires. In addition, these ideas are reinforced by the narrative's sexual vocabulary, *chker* and *nker* (Abn Manzur, n.d.), used metaphorically to describe the inhaling and exhaling of the historical seductress Ayesha, daughter of Talha, and one of her husbands during sexual intercourse. The same thing can be said about Wiladah, daughter of Al-Mustakfi, who defied religious and social taboos by generously making her body available to all of her lovers ("to anyone who desired it").

The narrative reaches another climax when the heroine, under the influence of wine but at the same time still fearful, feels the need to lock herself in her own bedroom in order to express her cultural alienation (coma) and refuse her Arab affiliation:

> She laughed while she was dancing and spun herself around after she locked her bedroom door forcefully. "Ya Salaam. . ." [Oh, God]. All the male Sudanese know about Arab women is that they wrap themselves in black abayas and engage in polygamy, with several of them being married to one man. (p. 91)

The narrative reveals a sarcastic attitude about the ignorance of Sudanese men about the reality of Arab women through Nasra's wine-intoxicated consciousness. Clearly, the voice of the narrator, united with Nasra's interior monologue, declare together, "Certainly, she is not Arab. . . . She doesn't have the capacity to carry all this physical and spiritual heritage" (91). She disassociates herself from her Arab identity that has become a heavy legacy and painful memory. At this moment, the narrative requires

Nasra's African heritage as an alternative that provides her dignity instead of humiliation.

In the following excerpt, Nasra proudly declares her African roots by shaking from her body the dust of Arab affiliation. Furthermore, the reader can interpret the black novelist's voice supporting Nasra:

> She is Tajoj's granddaughter. She is the granddaughter Nasra Adlan, a legendary princess whose story was expunged and whose life is part of the untold history of Sudan. Nasra Adlan was a strong, wise, beautiful princess who did everything that the male king did, and she enjoyed her life to the extremes of pleasure. She was brave and bold in expressing her opinion. Her biography includes many interesting stories. She [the protagonist Nasra] is named after Nasra Adlan. Perhaps if her mother (Al Hajah Zaharah) had known about Nasra's name, she would have chosen another name for her daughter. Thank God . . . She had not known . . . She admires this name very much. She [the protagonist Nasra] recalled vividly the rapturous tones and rhythms of tambourines, which swirled about her mind along with stories of the legendary Nasra Adlan, which she read in the National Archives Center in Khartoum. She started dancing, dancing . . . and spun herself around until she fell to the ground unconscious from the intensity of emotion (pp. 91-93).

This excerpt brings to the reader the legendary African princess Nasra Adlan, a beautiful, strong, and wise black woman, as a psychological equivalent for the suffering protagonist Nasra, providing her with a strong alternative identity after she has stripped away what seems to her to be the absurdity of her Arab identity. This discarded Arab identity is essentially an ankle bracelet of thorns that shackles Nasra, making her less that human, a member of a slave class, because of her black skin. The scene pits Nasra, an undefined female protagonist, against two powers. The first is her mother, Al Hajah Zaharah, a guardian of Arab masculine culture who had she known would not have named her daughter after a black woman powerful enough to rule over men. The second power is cultural, political, and historical ignorance ("story was expunged and whose life is part of the untold history of Sudan"). These two powers support each other to imprison rebellious Nasra, who rejects her cultural, social, and religious Arab affiliation. In fact, these powers have such combined strength that they reduce the intoxicated, wildly dancing Nasra to unconsciousness. There are many possible interpretations of this scene. One of them reminds us of Sufi ceremonies under the influence of spiritual wine and the tambourine, which feature dervishes, dancing, and spinning, to release the believers from their bodies to connect and unify with the highest power. Nasra's dancing under the influence of wine and rhythmic tambourines is not a ceremony of happiness; instead, she drinks, dances intoxicatedly, and spins and spins to try to release herself from the suffering caused by her female body and her black skin. This is a new, black, female dervish; however, it is bitterly ironic because it does not end in ecstatic union but instead with unconsciousness. Nasra cannot escape her reality.

The following excerpt weaves two black voices: Nasra's, through interior monologue, and Makki's, through the narrator. In this scene, wine offers Nasra a safe journey within her inner self, without religious and social censorship. It is a journey away from judgment and taboos. However, such a journey cannot be made in a conscious state, especially since the novel's audience is Arab:

> The fragrance of wine assaulted her nostrils while she was shaking the bottle unconsciously contemplating the golden liquid inside, following the drift of her ideas about what Al-Buhturi said, or perhaps he was Ibn Al-Rumi? She cursed all Arab poets, and she remembered how the Sudanese poet Mohommad Al-Mehedi Al-Majzoub tried to break free from his Arab constraints that cling to the African race and made himself free through pleasure and joy. He was a Muslim poet with a Sufi spirit and has a fantastic poem about the birth of the prophet, but he also says: *I wish were in a negro group and had my own rabab / I follow the rabab's music in my zigzagging steps / I ask him, and he is shocked and complains exactly as a person feverish with pain / I swallow al-marisa (wine) in the alley and I speak deliriously and no one blames me and I don't blame anyone / I am freestanding and neither the Quraish nor the Tamim can constrain me by a great lineage / I will be murdered in the road and in my eyes the mist of intoxication and wanton rapture.* But Al-Majzoub is a man, and men in al'aerab [Bedouin] society are free, and he can do what he wants, even if it violates legitimate and civil laws (pp. 87-89).

The wine acts as a stimulus of two crises: the first is racial, and the second is feminist. The racial crisis is the crisis of black skin, which makes the protagonist strip away her Arab poetic memory when she recalls the poets Al-Buhturi and Ibn Al-Rumi, who present the highest level of legendary poetry but then dismisses the thought when "She cursed all Arab poets." This cursing of Arab poets is her realization that there is a psychological separation between herself and the Arab poetic memory that she had erroneously thought was hers. As a cultural alternative, Nasra calls upon her African poetic memory, which belongs to her color and history. This alternative poetic figure is the rebellious and cynical black Sudanese poet Mohommad Al-Mehedi Al-Majzoub, who repudiates his Arab affiliation with the lines "I am freestanding and neither the Quraish nor the Tamim [two tribes that are root of Arabism] can constrain me by a great lineage." The other crisis, which is located at the end of the scene, is when Nasra feels her female identity under the influence of the Arab patriarchal culture and its taboos that allow men what is prohibited for women, which is described by Nasra as "al'aerab [Bedouin] society" (not Arab societies) to strip from the Arab societies civil status and civilization.

Mahjoub: Black Male Protagonist

The other protagonist in the novel is a young Sudanese black man named Mahjoub, who goes to Saudi Arabia for Umrah [a pilgrimage to Mecca at any time of the year] and then decides, under his ambitious wife's urging, to stay in Saudi Arabia to work, only to find himself on a journey inside the heart of darkness and nightmare which takes him to the horizon of slavery again. Indeed, Mahjoub endures a double journey: the first explicitly religious; the other implicit, in the womb of the social culture of Arab identity. This second journey gives him only a sense of humiliation and a memory wounded forever, which reflects the novel's title, *Ankle Bracelet of Thorns*.

The following excerpt from the novel highlights the details of the meeting between black, university-educated Mahjoub and Adnan al-Salhi, a Saudi entrepreneur who promises Mahjoub, after verification of Mahjoub's credentials, an opportunity to find a job and alleviate his financial crisis. The text reveals the details of a journey that is horrifically different from Mahjoub's spiritual pilgrimage for Umrah, a journey into the heart of the dark Arab desert that returns him to the reality of the Arab mindset that classifies black Arabs at a low social status that dehumanizes them and puts them at the level of cattle and animals. As an example, the following excerpt describes the beginning of Mahjoub's unexpectedly nightmarish journey:

In a small pickup truck carrying cattle, Adnan Al-Salhi encouraged him to get in quickly. . . . He opened the passenger-side door, but the man encouraged in him a harsh voice, "Get in back, bro. Right in the back." Then Adnan opened the driver's-side door, got in behind the wheel, and slammed the door. Mahjoub looked around him in humiliation, and rolled up his left trouser leg to get into the back of the truck. He almost fell on his face when the truck suddenly lurched into motion. The thick blood roared in his veins when he discovered a black female goat with thick fur and twin offspring while a thin ewe lay on the floor of the truck bed. The black goat looked at him with aggressive eyes and started bleating pleadingly as if with a strange person who was trespassing. Mahjoub stood up feeling humiliation and degradation and flagellating himself inside, which he had been addicted to since had had left his homeland. Mahjoub kept standing there, and the black goat kept bleating, and other goats responded to her bleating. However, the ewe expressed her dissatisfaction mockingly by wagging her tail and beginning to defecate. The sloppy and wormy feces assaulted his nostrils and flowed over and around his feet (p. 15).

This excerpt exposes the way that Arab culture treats black Arabs and how they judge them by their skin color, stripping from them an Arab history they share with white Arabs. This culture is exemplified by the character Adnan Al-Salhi, whose first name, Adnan, refers to the ancient Arab tribe which lives in Al-Jazirah and Al-Hijaz, and his last name, Al-Salhi, means "a righteous person." Adnan is a mirror that reflects a culture that shackles black Arabs into the class of servants and slaves, from which they cannot escape. A prime example of this Adnan's shock when Mahjoub tries to share with him the front seat of the pickup and Adnan's anger at what he perceives as effrontery from a black man, even though Mahjoub's relegation to the back of the truck leaves a passenger seat empty of the entirety of the trip. The contrast between the white Arab master and the black Arab slave is made clear by Mahjoub's confinement with the animals, which is seen as the natural place for a black man. In this way, the text highlights the nature of racial discrimination that strips black Arabs of their humanity and confronts the reader with the contrast between the human master and the animalistic slave.

The following excerpt highlights Mahjoub's bitter feelings, which reach the climax of his surrender to his fate and the contrast between the owner (the white character, Adnan Al-Salhi) and the slave (the black character, Mahjoub). This happens in a nightmarish setting that makes the Arab desert symbolic of the Arab identity as mute witness. This scene reveals Mahjoub's need to balance the horror of his present situation with warm memories from his childhood. It is a psychological coping mechanism to assert his humanity:

> He [Mahjoub] remembered the shepherd who came every day to his small town and knocked on the door of his house with a stick with a special knock which distinguished him from other intruders, and his mother started calling his sister and encouraging her to release the five goats. . . . He remembered how on one occasion his mother ordered him to release these goats when his sister was sick with chicken pox. He was attacked violently by a frightening smell while he has trying to release the second goat, so he began to vomit harshly, frightening his mother [....]
>
> He started to exhale hot breath in a futile attempt to reject everything around him; he exhaled the dry hot air from his nostrils as if he were vomiting his soul.
>
> "Sit down. . . . Sit down."
>
> The driver hit the outside of the truck's door hard to alert him. (p. 16)

This excerpt shifts between to two time periods: Mahjoub's childhood with his loving mother and his current horrifying ordeal in the desert with Adnan. The two scenes have dark parallels: a servant, cattle, and a foul smell. Again the equation is made between Mahjoub (a black Arab) and animality.

The narrative continues, and Mahjoub's surrender to his slavery fate reaches its climax in the following scene:

> Suddenly he awoke to the disappearance of mountains and shadows. The vehicle trampled the road in the full darkness of the frightening desert, and the goat smells crowded the hot air that attacked his face and his nostrils. The vehicle suddenly stopped, and he heard the front door open, expecting something evil.
>
> What if this Bedouin is a terrorist and intends to slaughter him?
>
> Certainly his blood will be shed then disappear in the desert and no one will hear about it!!
>
> The steps of the man advance toward him as he tries to hold onto himself and expel the fear.
>
> "Did you sleep, my Bro?"
>
> He did not respond and remained silent.

The man said speculatively, "O Sudanese, what's wrong with you. . . . Are you asleep?"

"No. . . ."

One word he said in his coarseness as he tried to push away from himself all the evil man's intentions that he imagined. (pp. 18-19)

The text here exposes the huge gap in status between Mahjoub, suffering the greatest intensity of his ordeal, reduced to the status of cattle, and Adnan, who has an inferior view of Mahjoub, calling him "O Sudanese" and presuming that since Mahjoub is sleeping with cattle that is where he belongs. Mahjoub's interior monologue reflects that Adnan is the owner of the cattle and Mahjoub himself. However, this is not the end of the nightmarish atmosphere. Mahjoub realizes with terror that he is completely in Adnan's power. Adnan, whom Mahjoub refers to as "Bedouin," could slaughter him like a sheep. The setting is the desert, a symbol of all that is good in Arab culture, but here it will be a mute witness to bloodshed.

The following excerpt reveals the cultural connection between black skin and slavery, and the career that belongs to slaves in the Arab cultural mindset. This appears through a one-sided dialogue by Adnan:

"I say to you, O Sudanese. . . . So we are going to reach the checkpoint. If someone asks you, tell them you are my shepherd. . . . Do you understand me. . . ? Tell the police officer you have been working under my authority for two years and that your job is to clean up the stable and feed the cattle."

Shameful sweat exploded in Mahjoub's scalp. He remained silent, so the man set a job for him at this moment on this wild night in this dark, locked desert. Mahjoub thought in his worst predictions that his job would not be below an editing or accounting job. To work as a shepherd did not occur to his mind at all. (p. 19)

The structure of this scene is symbolic of the relationship between the two characters. The white master barks orders while the black slave must obey silently: "He remained silent." However, Mahjoub, proceeding with his inner voice, here reveals the depths of spatial and psychological alienation when he finds himself confined inside the stereotype of black Arabs and the nature of their careers. This is a shattering moment in Mahjoub's long journey, which reflects the Arab mindset from past to present. The desert, symbolic of Arab values, appears "dark" and "locked" to reflect the depth of separation between Mahjoub, a black Arab, and the symbolic Arabism when it becomes a dismal, hostile place.

The following excerpt highlights Mahjoub's conscious decision not to respond to Adnan's insults:

"O Bro, aren't you hearing? I swear if you don't like my words, you can step down now and you can walk on your way because I don't want you to start your crazy Sudanese behavior."

Mahjoub did not respond. . . .

The Bedouin emphasized. . . . "I don't know what's in the air that pushed me to bring you with me. . . . Even I know the Sudanese stubbornness!! Oh Allah, we do not ask you to adjust or modify your fate, but to be courteous to us."

"Alas, Sheikh, don't be mad, everything you said will be!"

He imagined that the man's features, which were hidden in

the darkness, became elated.

"All right." (p. 20)

Obviously, the number of insults to Mahjoub by Adnan expose hidden though culturally accepted stereotypes of black Arabs. In this scene, Mahjoub has two bitter options: stay as a shepherd or leave to die in the dark desert.

The following scene highlights the common social categories to which people are consigned in Arab culture. The policeman speaks for political power, Adnan speaks for social power, and Mahjoub is relegated to the status of animal:

> Ten minutes later, the driver turned all the truck's lights on, stopped at the checkpoint, and stepped down from the vehicle.
>
> "What's up, man? Why are you traveling during the night?"
>
> His Arabic language was reined in and his phrases full of suspicion. "I—God give you long life—have worked at the town and I arrived late and night fell."
>
> "Who's with you in the truck?"
>
> The police officer at the checkpoint shined a strong light from his flashlight at a goat's eyes and her kids', and then stopped on Mahjoub, who was dazzled by the strong light in his eyes. The police officer turned the light toward the ewe . . But he returned with his flashlight to Mahjoub.
>
> "Who is he?"
>
> "This is a servant. He is working for me in the stable. . . . He takes care of the goats and cleans the place up." The words fell like the blow of a cruel mallet on Mahjoub's head, his body started to tremble, and he felt a high fever like fire.
>
> "What's wrong with him? Is he sick??
>
> The Bedouin's eyes widened. . . . "No. . He's OK. Nothing wrong with him. Maybe he's tired. . . . Or asleep. . . . Those Sudanese people are so lazy."
>
> The policeman stood up and turned off his flashlight, saying, "It's necessary to take him to the health center for a periodic examination. I'm afraid he could carry a disease, and he could infect you and your family."
>
> "Allah reward you."
>
> The policeman went to his seat, and the Bedouin got in his truck, put it in drive, and the truck entered the darkness of night, so Mahjoub was dizzy, spun around, and fell like an unknown corpse on the bed of the truck. He didn't care about the feces, the ewe, or the smells of the goats and sheep.
>
> The blade entered to the hilt in his breast. His body poured onto the ground . . . on his dignity, his mind, his soul, while his dignity lay suffering beneath him. (p. 21)

This scene exposes the nightmarish situation and the hostile vision against Mahjoub, who is robbed of his humanity because of his black skin: he is a "servant," in Adnan's words. Adnan, after all, puts him with the animals. The scene works on three levels: the policeman's, Adnan's, and Mahjoub's. The policeman's level is clear when he shines his flashlight between the goat and Mahjoub and sees nothing unusual in a black man being among the animals. Furthermore, the policeman views Mahjoub as a sick animal who is a threat to the health of others. Adnan's level is indicated by his placing

Mahjoub among the cattle and his referring to Mahjoub, "This is a servant. He is working for me in the stable. . . . He takes care of the goats and cleans the place up." This highlights the common lot of blacks in conventional Arab society. Mahjoub's level is his physical trembling and eventual fainting in reaction to the overpowering humiliation of his situation, feeling so abased that he doesn't mind the animal stench and filth he lies in. The imagery ("the blade entered to the hilt") shortly after this points to a metaphorical death for Mahjoub.

The novel reinforces in many places the nature of the acute class differences between the white master's life of "white villas surrounded by date-palm forests" and the place of black Mahjoub, late in the novel, in his stable:

> Mahjoub awoke, surprised that he had been asleep in the back of the truck, with a sense of foreboding pulling hard at his exhausted mind and rousing his memory. He sat up, feeling his head with his two hands, and he looked around to see a group of houses surrounded by white houses and colorful villas surrounded by forests of palm trees. His hand felt the place where he had been sleeping, and he was shocked by the dried urine and feces that had been his bed. He raised his head and inhaled the strong fragrance of the desert (p. 99).

The following excerpt clarifies the deep psychological conflict inside the hero, which leads him to feelings of depression and isolation:

> From that day, had been working under the authority of Adnan Al-Salihi, but after twenty-four months, he hated the place and refrained from food or speech. His master noticed this; therefore, he paid him off for his work and exempted him from service. (p. 99)

The novelist's use of the word "master" makes clear the relationship between Al-Salihi and Mahjoub. In fact, Al-Salihi's payment and dismissal of Mahjoub is not an act of kindness but rather of convenience; he does not want a dead servant on his hands. Furthermore, Mahjoub's refusal of food and speech is an act of protest against the unfair life he has been living. This excerpt reminds the reader of the wretched status of the slave-class life in Arab culture.

The next excerpt highlights the depth of wound left by the strenuous journey when the hero's consciousness denies the painful details when he remembers a hint of its own relevance:

> When he arrived at Khartoum, he told his wife and his friends that he was working as an accountant in a commercial office in Tabuk, and he was evading his memories of his work in the livestock barn. But one day, in a fit of madness, he almost tried to burn some of the money that he had earned in the stables as he was counting it. To him, the dollars smelled of dung and the feed of camels. (p. 99)

This excerpt illuminates the depth of the bleeding wounds and the resultant scarring of Mahjoub's psyche. It makes the money an eyewitness to the shame and degradation of his experience in the stables. Furthermore, the mention of the camel, a positive moral symbol of Arabism, is ironic in this case, because it becomes for black Mahjoub a symbol of shame and humiliation.

The following novelistic scene is accompanied by the aggravation of Mahjoub's psychological crisis and the exposure of his suffering when he is overcome by the wounded memory of his loss of dignity:

> And he was happy to see the day that he would get rid of the stinking dollars that he was putting under the bed; he sometimes imagined the smells of animal droppings, so he asked his wife to burn sandalwood incense, and to make more, to cover the smell of the money. This confused her; before his travels, he despised the scent. (p. 100)

In this excerpt, the incense represents the first intimate place that fails to escape the shame of Mahjoub's memory, which is humiliated and insulted when its relation to the dollars obtained from his work reflects the state of nausea and revulsion at its past.

Finally, the novel *Ankle Bracelet of Thorns*, by Buthaina Khuder Makki, succeeds in highlighting the phenomenon of racial discrimination against Black Arabs in the Arab world, and does so through narrative techniques that approach folklore texts, with a hero and a heroine who each experience double journeys, the first religious and the second cultural. Both Nasra and Mahjoub undergo a journey, a religious pilgrimage to Mecca. This journey reinforces the spiritual side of what is a holy place in Saudi Arabia. The other journey is cultural, which is going through the deepest level of the Arab mindset. Nasra's journey is through her Arab poetic memory and her intellectual affiliation to Arabism through her unconscious when she becomes intoxicated on the wine she drinks and passes out. Mahjoub's journey is through the deep Arab desert, which is symbolic of Arab culture and its spiritual mindset. Like Nasra, Mahjoub loses consciousness under the highest level of stress and pressure, which results in his returning to Sudan injured and humiliated. During each of their journeys, the protagonists lose their consciousness inside the nightmare of racial crisis, making them unable to escape.

References

Abn Manzur. (n.d.). *Lisan al-Arab*. Beirut, Lebanon: Dar Sader.

Al-Mutanabi, A.A. (n.d.). *Collected poems*. Vol. 3. Edited with commentary by F. Dietersby. Beirut, Dar Sader.

Afra Abdel Rahman in the hour dialogue with Buthaina Khader Makki. (2013, May 30). *YouTube*. Posted by Sudanese Online.

Al-Zuzani. A.A.A. (2013). *Explanation of the seven pendants*. N.p.

Antarah. (1994). *Collected poems [Diwan antar]*. Second edition. Commentary by K. Tabrizi. Verified and edited by M. Trad. Beirut, Lebanon: Lebanese Book House.

Kathem, N. (2004). *Representations of the other: The image of blacks in the Arab mediator*. Bahraini Ministry of Media, Culture, and National Folklore. Beirut, Lebanon: Arab Institution for Studies and Publishing.

Labbe. T. (2004, January 11). A legacy hidden in plain sight. *The Washington Post*. Retrieved from http://www.washingtonpost.com/wpdyn/content/article/2004/01/11/AR2005032403999.html

Mamouri, A. (2013, June 26). Black Iraqis struggle to shake
  legacy of racism. Translated by S. Abboud. *Iraq Pulse*. Retrieved
  from http://www.almonitor.com/pulse/originals/2013/06/black-
  iraqis-face-discrimination-racism.html

Makki, B. K. (2004). *Ankle bracelet of thorns*. Khartoum, Sudan: Dar Al Sidra
  Printing, Publishing, and Distribution.

Tabrizi, K. (n.d.). *Explanation of the ten poems*. Investigation by
  M.M. Abdul Hamid. Cairo: Mohammed Ali Sabeeh Library and
  Sons.

Thabit, H.B. (1994). *Collected poems*. Second edition. Explanation and
  presentation by Abd Mohanna. Beirut, Lebanon: Scientific Book
  House, p. 222.

CHAPTER 3

ARAB WOMEN'S WRITING
AND SOCIAL AND CULTURAL TABOOS:
HUDA AL-ATTAS

(1)

Women Writers in Yemeni Society

Yemeni society is a community teeming with contradictions. In
development, it ranges from urbanization to extreme underdevelopment. In
human rights, it ranges from maximum tolerance to extreme oppression
and marginalization. In independent wealth, it ranges from extreme wealth
to extreme poverty and hunger. Most importantly, in women's rights, it
ranges from extreme enforcement of the *niqab* and the *burqa* to the
unveiling and taking off of such veils and also from extreme patriarchy and
honor killing to the maximum freedom and rights of women to make their
own decisions, own their own businesses, choose a spouse, and drive a car
and travel without a *mahram* [male guardian].

Despite these contradictions, the majority of people in Yemeni
cities, despite the lack of modern infrastructure because of governmental
corruption, hold a civilized view of women and women writers, often
featuring these writers without veils (and sometimes without scarves) on the
covers of newspapers and magazines and in television interviews. The
writings of women that courageously confront social, political, and religious
topics are featured prominently in the front of newspapers. Some of these
acclaimed writers, such as poet, journalist, and novelist Nabelah Al-Zubair,
born in 1964, whose novel *It Is My Body* (2000), winner of the Naguib
Mahfouz Prize, provoked outrage in the streets of Cairo. Another
prominent female author, short story writer, folklore activist, and journalist
Arwa Abdah Othman, born in 1965, does not wear a *hijab* in public. She is
the founder of the Yemeni Folklore House and encourages dancing and
singing, which are prohibited in public. Her short story collection, *It Is
Happening in Tanaka, Nams Homeland* (2001), was awarded the Creative
Writing Award from the Cultural Ministry of the UAE, Dubai. She has
been appointed as the first writer and the first female cultural minister in
Yemen.

The poet Huda Ablan's (born in 1971) collection *Half-bow* (1997)
received the Creativity of Women Award in Sharjah, the capital of Arab
culture, in 1998. She was elected as the first secretary-general of the Union
of Writers, the first woman to hold this position, and is currently the
Deputy of the Ministry of Culture. The novelist and short-story writer Dr.
Nadia Kawkabani's (born in 1968) collection *Jasmine Sigh* (2001) won the
Suad Al-Sabah Prize for Young Writers in Kuwait, in 2000. She serves as a
professor in the Faculty of Engineering, University of Sanaa. Journalist,
writer, and political activist Tawakul Karman, born in 1979, was awarded
the Nobel Peace Prize in 2011 and gained unprecedented popular support
from Yemeni society.

Looking back to the 19th century, we find the poet Ghazaleh
Almekdhah endorsed by Yemeni tribes in the Ottoman era to be the first

tribal poet discussing tribal affairs, calling for equality between men and women, and being consulted by tribal elders to resolve the political problems that beset the region at the time. Even earlier, we encounter Arwa Sulayahiah, nicknamed "the Free Lady," the only Islamic queen, who ruled and established the Sulayhid dynasty. Earlier yet, we have Bilquis, the Queen of Sheba, about whom there are many religious taboos, such as the Prophet Mohammed's injunction, "God damned the people that allowed a woman to govern them."

But this did not change Yemeni society. Actually, most liberal, educated Yemeni men are proud of women's achievements and have even backed their creative endeavors and their stand against the marginalization of women and against the patriarchy. For example, the former Prime Minister, Mohsen Alainy, supports his wife, novelist Azizah Abd Allah, born in 1945. Furthermore, her fifth novel, *My Father's Wedding* (2004), discusses controversial religious and social issues, particularly polygamy. In addition, the poet and former Secretary General of the Writers Union, Mohammed Hussein Haitham, supported his daughter, novelist Hind Haitham, who discussed in her novel *The War of Wood* (2003) the social taboo and culture of tribal revenge. The poet Ibrahim Elhoudrani, former Ambassador to Kuwait, supported his daughter Dr. Bilqis Elhoudrani, a political writer, professor at Sanaa University, and opposition party leader. Ahmed Jaber Afif, founder of the first university in Yemen, former Minister of Education, and founder of the Afif Cultural Foundation, is eager to present his wife at foundation events and keeps his commitment to honoring women's writing. Similarly, iconic Yemeni poet Dr. Abdulaziz Al-Maqaleh, winner of numerous awards, including the Arab Culture Prize, UNESCO (2002), and the Knight of the First Class in Arts from the French government in 2003, head of Sanaa University, and head of the Yemeni Center for Studies of Writers, encourages and supports a new generation of women writers by introducing their work in the press, in printed books, and in other media.

Furthermore, many factors encourage Yemeni society to appreciate writing and writers. In fact, it is common day and night to see street libraries in Yemeni cities lined with people reading and buying books at low prices. In addition to this, many publishing houses, whether privately owned, university affiliated, or sponsored by the cultural ministry, greatly facilitate the printing and distribution of books. In addition, newspapers provide a forum for freedom of speech for men and women, even dissenting views. Cultural institutions, whose programs are well attended, sponsor opportunities for writers to be published in elegant editions, increase public appreciation for the arts, contain large free libraries, and offer many annual prizes for writers of all genres. Just a few of these institutions include the Creativity Foundation in Sanaa, founded by the poet and Ambassador to Cairo Abdul-Wali al-Shamiri; Foundation Al-Afif, founded by Ahmed Jaber Afif; the Al-Saeed Foundation in the Taiz, run by businessman Hail Saeed Anam; the Al-Hewar [Dialogue] Foundation in Dhamar, founded by novelist and short story writer Muhammad Imran, better known by his adopted middle name, Al-Gharbi, which means "Western man." These institutions' activities are frequently standing-room-only events.

On the other hand, we find a frightening decrease in the level of government services, where in most Yemeni villages the most basic services are absent. Also absent, due to poverty and ignorance, are women's rights. Tribal revenge, honor killings, child marriage, and a patriarchal system are the norm. In the cities as well, governmental corruption and poverty are common, resulting in child labor, networks that employ children to beg in the streets, and child prostitution, among other social ills.

A temporary marriage (*nikah misyar*) victimizes young virgin girls from poor families and sells them for a night to Saudi men (before the recent war between Yemen and Saudi Arabia). A scene commonly present in poor neighborhoods was the presence of an expensive car parked in front of a very poor house.

Moreover, there are other phenomena that exist in the complete absence of law enforcement and the implementation of its provisions and because of the prevalence of administrative corruption. As a result, political jokes grow and reflect the terrible conditions that are so prevalent. The Yemeni environment allows the free expression of these jokes to extend even to the president and his government. For example, Ali Abdullah Saleh, the former president, wrote to the US government stressing that al-Qaeda are present in Yemen and assuming that money would be the first response. However, the US government offered him military assistance to fight terrorism in Yemen. He said, "No, no, thank you guys, but just give me money, and I'm going to take care of them." These jokes sometimes criticize the corruption in the Yemeni universities, especially the administrators who gain financial advantage from the donor nations. For example, the people of the city of Dhamar have jokes about the first president of Dhamar University, who amassed huge amounts of money from donor countries for the new university. However, when he got the money, all he did was lengthen a fence surrounding the empty area. The Dhamari people named this wall the Great Wall of Dhamar University in an ironic analogy to the Great Wall of China. Such contradictions have rocked the humanitarian scene as well as the cultural scene, especially when death sentences (*fatwa*) and *hadr al-dhamm* ("his blood can be spilled") against writers are made by imams upon the stages of mosques during the Friday religious speeches. For example, after the novelist Wijdi Ahdal, born 1973, published his 2002 novel *Mountain's Boats*, he faced the serious charge of insulting the divine due to the novel's discussion of social and religious taboos. The fatwa against him was made by imams. As result, a subsequent alliance between the political and religious powers was demonstrated by the banning of the novel and the closure of the Yemeni Publishing House that published the novel and the prosecution of its owner, Mohammed Abdul Latif Ebadi, and Ahdal in a judicial trial on charges of insulting traditional Yemeni values.

This led to Ahdal fleeing the country and fearing to return. Enter novelist Gunter Grass (winner of the Nobel Prize), who, during his 2004 visit to Yemen to attend a literary conference, refused to receive an honorary medal from President Ali Abdullah Saleh unless he promised to drop all charges against Ahdal and secure his return to Yemen protected. This put the Yemeni president in an awkward position, so he had no choice but to accept Grass's terms. Before Ahdal was expelled, poet Mohammed Sharafi (1940 - 2012), known as "the woman's poet" and former ambassador in Iraq, endured the same double punishment. Because his plays and poems called for the liberation of women and the disposal of the *niqab* (veil), he was dismissed from his governmental job and denounced by the imams as an infidel, and a fatwa was pronounced.

It is worth mentioning that the Arab Spring may cast a shadow clearly on the Yemeni creative scene, specifically feminist writers. Most writers have turned into political activists, are leading demonstrations, and are announcing their views to the media. These writers-turned-activists have gained many followers and supporters. It was during the Arab Spring that one woman writer, Arwa Othman, rose to the position of Minister of Culture.

Currently, these Yemeni women writers, as well as a whole new generation, are thriving despite horrifying circumstances. Since 2005, war and airstrikes have raged in Yemen, resulting in famine, diseases (such as cholera), food shortages, no medicine, no financial infrastructure, and no water or electricity. However, Yemeni women writers continue to create their own paradise by publishing their writing (even though they are not paid for it), earning national and international awards, and actively presenting at literary events. Yemeni women writers resist daily distractions by writing, which is their refuge, their only window on living.

Huda Al-Attas: A Writer Who Speaks for the Unheard Women of Yemen

Yemeni short story writer and journalist Huda Al-Attas, born in 1971, is a pioneer of women's short-story writing in Yemen and other Arab countries. She is known as a liberal advocate of human rights and equality between people. She was well known before the Arab Spring as a brave and bold writer who shed light on religious, social, sexual, and political taboos in a conservative society that shackle both men's and women's rights and prevent progress. She has received awards from many different Arab countries, such as Yemen and the UAE. Her collections of short stories include *Obsessed Spirit . . . Obsessed Body* (*hājis rūh wa hājis jasad*, 1995), *Because She* (*li'annaha*, 2001), and *Lightning Training to Be Light* (bariq yatadarrab alada', 2003). Her work has been translated into many languages. Topics that she addresses include incest, patriarchal ownership of women's bodies, child brides, child begging, child labor, khat addiction, and tribal revenge, to name a few. She explores these topics through innovative literary techniques that are as liberating as her subject matter. One of these literary techniques is projection: a Jungian concept that employs natural phenomena, living and not living, as symbolic mirrors of her characters.[1]

A good example of her projection technique is her story "Whining," from her collection *Because She*, which illuminates patriarchal practices through the phenomenon of *alqatl ghaslaan lilear* (honor killing.) Al-Attas highlights the tragedy of her heroine, Safia, by mirroring her surrender to patriarchy with the image of a hen. Here is the beginning of the story:

> When Safia put the last hen in the cage, her ear caught the muezzin of the mosque next door clearing his throat, and she inhaled the fragrance of the sunset breeze and said to herself, "This should be the perfume of the male newcomer from the city whom everyone is talking about." (38)

The identification between the heroine and the hen suggests several things. The first is that, like the hen, Safia is caged. Also like the hen, Safia is naïve to the point of stupidity. Indeed, like a hen, she does not understand her situation and walks unwittingly to her tragic end. The reader should also bear in mind that *safia*, in Arabic, means "pure."

Later in the story, Al-Attas employs further projection techniques when Safia meets the man:

> Safia balanced the jar filled with water on her head and took a tiring walk through the winding paths of the small village. When she heard the braying donkey coming, she moved away a bit from the road to avoid it. She raised her eyes shyly, then suddenly she opened them very widely. He was the newcomer from the city riding a donkey and face to face in front of her. She was nailed in place, her astonishment froze her feet to the ground. . . . She stared

[1] "As we know, it is not the conscious subject but the unconscious which does the projecting. Hence one meets with projections, one does not make them. The effect of projection is to isolate the subject from his environment, since instead of a real relation to it there is now only an illusory one. Projections change the world into the replica of one's own unknown face." –Carl Jung, *Aion*, p. 9

at him, and he stared back, his nostrils filled with the smell of the earth, the smell of wet mud just after the rain... and they remained staring at each other. Their wishes and their desires merged. The donkey brayed, and the wind carried the voices of cooing doves through the winding paths of the small village. (38-39)

In this scene, the cooing of the doves, suggesting Safia's purity, clashes with the braying of the donkey, which suggests the brute sexuality and stupidity of the man. By violating Safia, the man violates the patriarchal code that says a man should protect a woman. However, there is a double standard involved because the man (symbolically given no name in order to present the prevalence of the double standard) knows he can violate a woman's body with impunity. In fact, at the end of the story, the man starts his life with a lavish wedding party, whereas Safia's life is near its tragic end.

Later in the story, the projection technique becomes even more daring and intense when Safia is pregnant:

> After two months, Safia was writhing with pain and speeding to the bathroom to vomit and purge what she had eaten. Tears are fleeing from her eyes with a wish that she can empty her insides, even her intestines, hopefully expelling the balled creature inside her, and the pain is increasing, and writhing and clenching her teeth, she tries to loosen her dress so that it will not cleave to her abdomen. If not, the hidden will be shown.
>
> But the ruthless pain intensifies, like a sharp dagger, and she cannot control herself. She screams, and her mother rushes after it while her dress clings to the abdomen and the hidden is discovered. Like an injured wolf, the mother howled mournfully, reverberating throughout the house. (40)

Here, the projection of the injured wolf, a creature very dangerous to a hen, onto Safia's own mother suggests women's internalization of the patriarchal society. This influence is so strong that a mother would expose her daughter's shameful secret. As with the previous excerpt, no name is given to the antagonist—in this case, a woman guardian, who is actually more dangerous than the male in the patriarchal society depicted.

When the story reaches its climax, the reader finds further projection:

> In the night, the Ghost was jumping around Safia, who was curled up in one corner, receiving only the sounds of the knife being sharpened on a stone and the father clearing his throat, and she was listening carefully, hoping to catch the faintest sad and pitying tones from the throat clearing itself, but the father's face was festering with violence and pain, his hand sharpening the knife, making her lose hope . . . . and she shrank into herself, wanting to vanish. . . . She was stalked by dizziness and nausea and started to look with imbecility to the mother, who bowed her head with tears pouring, and to the father's masked face, who was sharpening the knife on the stone. The owl was screeching outside in the night, ghosts were jumping around her, a big ghost came closer to Safia. He came even closer and caught her braided hair and thunder shrieked, and a head was mowed, the blood bubbled and boiled on the ground and the victim's head with two braids and two eyes still open with a repressed question fell down. The injured wolf howled mournfully, the echo reverberating in the paths of the sadness (40).

Here, the "night ghosts" and owls outside are projections of the patriarchal culture in general; the "big ghost" is the father figure; and "the injured wolf" is the mother figure. Significantly, all of these creatures, unlike Safia, have the ability to flee. Safia is closed in—indeed, caged. The eerie darkness of this scene, with its reds and blacks, suggests a kind of *Guernica* for women in a patriarchal society.

In the story "Walls," from *Because She*, the projection technique highlights *zawaaj abn aleum* ("cousin's marriage"), a tribal patriarchal protocol that allots a young female's body among males. The specific image that Al-Attas employs is the heroine being a bird that is caged within the walls of a room. In fact, the heroine's name, Houria, means "female angel." Here are excerpts illustrating the projection technique:

> The bird's wings applauded, when suddenly, he found himself surrounded by the room . . . , forcibly or arbitrarily perhaps in his vision, like a dervish, he rose up reciting eulogies with his wings, and during his search for a large open window he crashed into the rough ceiling. . . . His wings applauded and his head began to butt the walls. "The heat coils around this morning," I said to myself. . . . Houria said from her inner corner seeded with weakness: "I will not marry my cousin," I murmured, "Don't marry him." I went back to record in my open-jawed diary. . . . Bird wings applauded, reeling across the four walls. Houria got up, opened the window for the bird, repeating "I will not marry my cousin," . . . but . . . the bird foundered, blind to the window, and remained flopping in the limited space.
>
> A hoarse voice called, "Houria, Houria" . . . ordering her to come down. She howled and whined heartbreakingly: "It's him," she hurried, wearing the black barrier over her head. The bird still butted his head hysterically against the walled space, and when he did not find his way the window, he plummeted, bloody, his battered wings snapped, crucified, to the floor. I got up, took him between my palms pitifully and painfully, and watched him go into an everlasting paralysis. (24-25)

The imagery reveals several similarities between Houria and the bird: both are caged and desperately unable to find a window; both plummet from a height when called by a patriarchal voice; both are covered (Houria in a black cloak, the bird in blood—black and red being a common color combination in Al-Attas's work); both are deprived of flight; and both die (the bird physically, Houria psychologically). This parallel symbolism is Al-Attas's condemnation of what is an essentially modern, metaphorical version of the pre-Islamic tradition of *wa'add albanat* (infanticide of female babies by being buried alive). Both Houria and the bird surrender to their fate.

The short story "Old Cut," from *Lightning Training to Be Light*, is about the suffering of young females under the patriarchal culture that demonizes the female by the practice of female circumcision, or female genital mutilation (FGM). Al-Attas bravely uses the name of a famous historical female in Islamic culture, Aisha, as a mask for her heroine:

> The night is quiet and Aisha steals away from the bed. ...
>
> While her husband demands her return to the bed, she is remaining in her special corner.

> His request pours down over her, she tries to sneak away. .
> . . When she can no longer elude him. . . She opens space in the
> body. . . He plunks down her rug, he thought she would take him
> far, far away, when he returns from his pleasurable trip, he asks
> about her trip:
>
> She remains silent. She hears him mutter, curse, and damn
> something. . . .
>
> He brings her sticks of coriander and says: to avail for the
> upcoming trips.
>
> Every day, in front of the mirror, she chews these sticks,
> watching her withered eyes and reflecting the memory within. . . .
>
> She was told that when she was an infant, just a ball of
> pink flesh, Umm Saber, Saber's mother, was approaching her and
> opening the space between her tiny thighs which were crossed to
> hide the mystery of mysteries—as she was told—this panacea of
> Heaven and Hell. Her scream precedes the swift blade, and the
> bubbling of blood and throwing away of the very small segment of
> the body's flesh. (98)

This might suggest the confusion in the contemporary Arab world over
whether FMG, the demonization of the female body, is a religious or a
cultural practice. This scene shuttles back and forth between present and
past, a marriage bed and an infant's cradle, between a sexually unfulfilled
couple and a female circumcision. In the scenes, there are three faces: two
victims (Aisha and her husband) and Umm Saber (mother of Saber), a
female who is a legitimatized guardian of oppressive masculine culture.
Aisha's husband is seeking an equal relationship with his wife, but finds her
body and soul demonized. In fact, he gives her *kazbra* (green coriander, a
traditional aphrodisiac) to help her with her next sexual journey. Umm
Saber enacts the bloody ceremony upon a pure female body which the
culture sees as a defiled body because it is intact sexually. Indeed, Aisha's is
the body around which the story is centered.

In the story "Cook," from Lightning Training to Be Light, Al-Attas
uses projection but also employs an innovative technique in her writing that
fuses fiction with the rich imagery and graphic form of the poem. The story
is set in a kitchen, a closed anti-patriarchal space to which women are
relegated, and the heroine is ostensibly preparing what appears on the page
to be just a recipe. However, this recipe elevates the heroine from her
slavish domestic role to that of a goddess:

> She decided to cook (Her Ego), she prepared her
> ingredients, she began to mix the dough (Ego):
>
> > a little bit of madness oil
> > a spicy ounce of rebellion
> > drops of vaporizing oils from the fruits of creativity
> > garlic cloves of wisdom, she added the good-hearted sauce
> > two horns of hot pepper of demonization
> > a colorless liquid called Angels' vinegar
> > she shed a teaspoon of the salt of common sense
>
> and mixed all of these in a pot (humanization), pouring the water
> of life over the dough, and she put it into the cosmic oven . . . and
> then she sat with apprehensive boredom and anxiety to wait. (30)

The heroine has innovatively transformed the kitchen, a space of female
ostracism, into a place of emancipation and liberation from the slavery

system of the patriarchy. Al-Attas uses the ingredients of the recipe, which is part of a woman's daily life, to comment with bitter irony on the status quo of her culture. Also notable is Al-Attas's innovative use of punctuation: she does not finish her sentences with periods but uses no punctuation in order to indicate the poetic, dynamic nature of the heroine's own self-creation. In addition, the blank space after each item in the recipe and especially the ellipsis mark before the last sentence invite readers to fill in their own experiences and impressions of a woman's painful daily routine. The story employs an open-ended technique that gives readers multiple interpretations. No one—heroine, reader, or writer—knows the end of the story.

In her story "Dewfall," from *Because She*, Al-Attas employs poetic intensification to tell the story of a woman's life, confined to the kitchen and the daily pain within its walls, in only two lines. This employs a prose-poem or flash-fiction technique that might remind readers of a haiku:

> Dewfall spoon was dancing in the center of the alfanjan (coffee cup). . . . As the sugar melted, the spoon lying in state, neglected (70).

Al-Attas uses the spoon as a projection technique, a metaphor for the woman, whose life moves from the splendor and freshness of her assigned role as a female ("dancing") to ostracism, exclusion, and ingratitude ("lying in state, neglected") after the expiration of her feminine seductiveness ('the sugar melted"). The ellipsis mark between the story's two sentences highlights the nature of a culture that transfers the heroine across these two realms. Using the teaspoon as a projection technique reflects bitter irony to condemn a masculine culture that uses the female body like a utensil and then discards it. Part of this irony is directed at women, many of whom are happy to perform their role perfectly while fully realizing that the patriarchal culture will discard them. One of Al-Attas's ironic techniques is to reverse the societal pattern of men being in the center and women being relegated to the margins. Her reversal puts her female characters at the center while relegating men to the margins. However, in "Dewfall," the irony is doubled because Al-Attas allows the reader the possibility that the unseen hand stirring the spoon and then setting it aside is the hand of either male patriarchy or female acquiescence.

Al-Attas's story "Camouflage," from *Obsessed Spirit . . . Obsessed Body*, interweaves the techniques of fiction with the semantic structure of the prose poem, all in order to capture the internal and external realities of women's lives:

> On the curtains, waves and depths and sea and a mermaid . . . and an octopus were drawn, and behind the curtains . . . sits the closed window (p. 31).

This story works with several ironic contradictory binaries: the depths of the sea depicted on the curtain versus the closed room; the mermaid versus the (female) narrator; the octopus versus the patriarchal power structure; the curtain versus the closed window. The biggest irony, however, is the "camouflage" itself: the beautiful curtain, seeming to offer freedom and life, simply hides a closed window: a bitter symbol of imprisonment.

The story "Stream" reflects the depths of sexual deprivation of the female culture through the use of prose poem and personification techniques. The female's masturbation in the first line of the poem defies social and religious taboos that forbid women from expressing their feelings, let alone their sexual needs:

Flowing nights. . . .
She closed her eyes; she married all men in the world. . . .
Her eyelids were thunderstruck when the cold bed opened its eyes.

(89)

The second line of the text gives the heroine of the story the absolute physical limit of freedom of sexual appetite through the ecstatic line "she married all men in the world." However, the third line makes clear oppressed women's cold, dark, dreary existence, through the personification of the cold bed that opens its eyes.

Huda al-Attas writes to and for women in stories that feature solitary female protagonists who speak for the unheard women in her society. She marginalizes men and mutes their voices to create her own narrative world that contradicts the reality of her culture, in which men occupy the center and speak with much louder voices than do women, who occupy the dark margins and whose voices are muted. In her stories, Huda al-Attas documents Arab women's lives in general and Yemeni women's lives in particular. However, in a broader sense, her work speaks to and for oppressed women everywhere. She does not cover women's bodies or their psychological and sexual feelings. She seeks to shake the dust from a culture that uses religion to constrain the role of women and their social interactions. Al-Attas boldly discusses topics that are very sensitive in the patriarchal system of conservative Arab society. In addition, she has created a new genre by interweaving the techniques of fiction, free verse, and the prose poem. It is not only her subject matter but also her literary techniques that embody the concept of liberation.

Works Cited

Al-Attas, Huda. *Because She* [*li'annaha*]. Al-Afif Cultural Foundation, Sana'a, 2001.

---. *Lightning Training to Be Light* [*bariq yatadarrab alada'*]. Yemen PressAgency: Saba, Sana'a, 2003.

---. *Obsessed Spirit . . . Obsessed Body* [*hājis rūh wa hājis jasad*]. Aden Ministry of Culture, Yemen, 1995.

Jung, C.J. *Aion: Researches into the Phenomenology of the Self*. 2nd ed, Translated by R.F.C. Hull. *The Collected Works of C.J. Jung*, volume 9, part II, https://archive.org/stream/collectedworksof92cgju/collectedwork sof92cgju_djvu.txt

CONCLUSION

This book has highlighted three Arab writers who have a prominent role in the Arab creative movement in general and the women's movement in particular. Despite their long creative history and their arduous journey of suffering as female writers, they fight in the name of women and for women in societies that deprive women of their most basic rights and consider women's voices sinful. Furthermore, in their societies, these women's writings compete bravely with men's over the public forum that writing provides.

These three writers have not been introduced to European-language readers by translation because they are outside the political agenda and media institutions, which are necessarily subordinate to the political agenda. This book is therefore the beginning of a series of studies that will shed light on creative women writers that have stood against taboos and discussed with courage the social and cultural issues that corner men and women to condemn them and deprive them of their basic right to express their opinions as individuals. These women writers demand social justice (freedom from cultural and religious taboos, racism, and patriarchal ideology) for men and women alike and seek to remove the social and cultural lipstick that beautifies ugly truths and the veils that hide the patriarchal practice and conceal the real facts.

This book focuses on fiction. Further projects will highlight several other writers of fiction and poetry. Indeed, there are many talented Arab women writers who, because of their feminism and resistance to the political and cultural agendas of their societies, are virtually unknown to European audiences. Among these women are fiction writers such as Nabila Zubair, Nadia Kokbani, Arwa Abdo Osman, Aziza Abdullah, Laila Othman, Hiyam Al-Mufleh, Arada Al-Jibouri, Huda Al-Nuaimi, Collette Khoury, and Latifia Al-Dulaimi; and poets such as Reem Qais Kubba, Fathia Ajlan, Saadia Mufarah, Huda Ablan, Eman Bakhri, Amal Mousa, and Rawdah Alhaj.

Dr. Wijdan Al-Sayegh, a well-known Arab writer, has over 16 years of experience in teaching and writing on Arabic literature and language. Her areas of expertise include: modern Arabic fiction, poetry, literary criticism, culture, and linguistics. She has published 24 books, three of which won renowned Arab prizes. Her first book, *The Rhetorical Imagery in Feminist Text* [*Al-Sura Al-Bayania fi Annass Al-nisaie' Al-Amarati*], won the Woman's Creations in Literature Award in Sharjah, 1998. Her book *The Throne and the Hoopoe: Rhetorical Analysis for Yemeni Poetry* [*Al-Arsh wa Al-Hudud*], won the Al-afeef Cultural Award for Literature and Arts in Yemen 2003. Her latest book is entitled *Shahrazad and Seductive Narration: Reading in Feminist Fiction* [*Shahrazad wa Ghuwayat al-Sard*], published by Dar Al-Uloom Publishers in Beirut and Algeria, 2008. Her publications deal with social, political, and religious taboos in modern Arabic texts. She has also been an active contributor to many Arabic journals, periodicals, and literary magazines across the Arab world.

Thomas Zimmerman teaches English, directs the Writing Center, and edits *The Big Windows Review* and *The Huron River Review* at Washtenaw Community College, in Ann Arbor, Michigan. He has over thirty years of teaching experience and has been active in the small press for over thirty years as well, publishing several hundred poems and earning Pushcart Prize, Best of the Net, Best Indie Lit New England, Rhysling Award, and Orison Anthology nominations. He is the author of seven poetry chapbooks, including *In Stereo* (Camel Saloon, 2012) and has received the Community College Humanities Association's Distinguished Humanities Educator Award. Tom's website: https://thomaszimmerman.wordpress.com/